7 Reasons Why You SUCK at Sales
&
What To Do About It

The Ultimate Guide to Stop Selling Like An Average Guy And Become One of The Great Instead

By William Wyatt

Disclaimer

The information provided in this book is designed to provide helpful information on the subjects discussed. The author's books are only meant to provide the reader with the basics knowledge of the topic in question, without any warranties regarding whether the reader will, or will not, be able to incorporate and apply all the information provided. Although the writer will make his best effort share her insights, the topic in question is a complex one, and each person needs a different timeframe to fully incorporate new information. This book, nor any of the author's books constitute a promise that the reader will learn anything within a certain timeframe.

Table of Contents

Final Words: It's Time To Get Out There And Make Something Happen!

Preview of "Alpha Male: Stop Being a P#ssy, Become an Alpha Male - The Ultimate Guide to Attract Women & Achieve Massive Success In Life"

Dedicated to those who love going beyond their own frontiers.

Keep on pushing,

William Wyatt

Introduction

Are You Ready To Become a Killing Sales Machine?

The contents of this book include things that you probably won't find with some of your run of the mill, generic sales books or articles. I'm not knocking sales books or sales teachers at all, there are a lot out there that do provide valuable content, but so many times we are so bombarded with generic statements about what we need to do to become successful in sales. This generic and monotonous view of the world of sales doesn't allow us to take the time to actually stop and understand what the real issues are or what we can do about them.

We hear over and over again that sales are a numbers game or that sales are an art form. That we need to stop being afraid of being rejected or that we need to understand the client on a deeper level. That we need to constantly be creating rapport with the client or that we need to deliver a memorable presentation. Most of these generic points are undoubtedly true, but they've become so darn generic that all we're doing is trying to find different viewpoints on the best way to do them. It's an ongoing and vicious cycle in which we ultimately end up learning very little about a certain topic. We relearn the same topic over and over again and never truly understand what it's going to take for us to take our sales to the next level in our career.

That's what this book was created for, to give you a look at some of the things that you've probably never thought about for what you need to do to get yourself on track. There's no BS here, and I'm not going to take it easy on you. This is a tough love guide for getting your sales career on the path you truly want it to be on. It's going to be personal, it's going to be in your face, and it's going to get your blood pressure going. It's time to sit down, figure out what's holding you back, and do something about it.

Many of you will read this and say that this guy thinks he knows everything. You'll say I'm an arrogant SOB that doesn't really know what I'm talking about. You'll want to see my credentials and ask if I even know what I'm doing or if I've even ever sold anything in my life. Well, to tell you the truth, I'm truly hoping this is your reaction. I'm hoping that you read through this with thoughts of writing a review about how arrogant and uninformed the author is.

This book is intended to get a rise out you. It's intended to touch on some emotions that very few sales teachings ever do. I want to get you thinking about sales in a way that you've never thought about it before. To be tough on you, but still give you ways that you can fix things and continue to help improve your career.

Sales aren't easy and I'm not sure that anybody ever really said it was. It's a challenging career to be involved in, which is why we get paid so much to do it. You need to be tough skinned and you need to be prepared to face the ups and downs that come with our world.

This isn't a book for the faint of heart. You will most likely be offended at some point. I'm not looking to provide you with generic statements that everybody's heard a million times. This is a tough love ride through a book that will hopefully revolutionize the way you think about your occupation.

Alright, enough with the warnings about how much this thing is going to rattle your emotions. It's time to buckle up and take you on a ride through the things that are holding us all back from achieving the type of success that we're all capable of reaching in our sales careers.

Reason #1

You SUCK Because You Fear Rejection

Yes, yes I know, I said this wouldn't be about generic statements and yet the first chapter is based on a generic statement that you've heard millions of times before. The purpose of this chapter isn't to tell you one more time that fearing rejection is holding you back, it's to give you a different perspective on what rejection should mean to you in your career.

Rejection is a huge part of our jobs as salesmen. It should be happening to us every single day of our career. If it's not, then we're probably not going to be very good at selling. Well that doesn't make any sense you say? Think of it this way, nobody that has ever been in sales has ever sold anywhere near a 100% clip over the long term. Aside from putting a gun to a potential client's head, there's no way you or anybody else is ever going to reach the level of closing 100% of your clients over a long period of time. It's not possible and it never will be.

Many of the greatest salesmen in the world will tell us that we should expect to be selling at a 10-20% clip. Now, obviously it depends on what we're selling and the amount that people are paying for the product but 20% is generally what we aim for as salesmen. As we continue to grow in our field hopefully that 10-20% begins translating into a 25-30% closing ratio, which is fairly phenomenal for any type of salesman.

So many people focus so deeply on improving and perfecting their presentation that they don't realize that most of the time it doesn't even matter how we present things. As long as we have a general idea of what we're doing people are eventually going to buy from us if we keep going. I know it's a hard concept to understand when we're struggling immensely and can't seem to do anything right. I know we just wish that we had that one little key thing to put us over the top but our occupation just simply doesn't work that way.

We need to stop spending so much time focusing on the presentation and learning the intricacies of the product or service you're selling. That's not going to get us anywhere. We need to be out in the field making things happen. The presentation that we give has little to do with the success we're going to have in the field. Taking action is the only thing that is going to change our current closing ratio and I can absolutely guarantee you that it's also the best way to improve our presentation.

So what can we do to change our views on rejection and stop fearing it as a whole? Well first of all, we need to realize that we're going to be scared. Being afraid of failure and rejection is something that is inundated into us from the beginning of our lives. The public education system is designed in a way that we are predestined to fear failure. There's nothing we can do about it at this point.

What we can do, however, is realize that we're going to be scared and fight through it anyhow. I've seen multiple times where people are so frozen by fear that they spend weeks, months, or even years finding a way to feel more comfortable in their sales situation. They'll constantly be searching for YouTube videos, online articles, or books that will show them what they need to do to become comfortable in their situations and stop being taken over by so much fear.

Most of these teachings will tell you that fear isn't real, that it's something you make up in your head. That's a bunch of BS. Fear is a part of life. Fear is always going to be a part of our lives and if it isn't then we aren't living our lives and improving ourselves the way we should be. Constantly doing things that we fear makes us who we are. It shows us that we can fight through uncomfortable situations and that we have what it takes to persevere through emotions that take over and destroy most people.

That isn't what you wanted to hear though was it? You were looking for that magic pill of advice that was going to allow you to stop being so darn scared of rejection. Well folks, there is none. Let me repeat once again, there is no magic pill. There's no magic potion, there's no magic anything. We fear and we act despite fear because we know where we want to go - the life and financial security that we want to have - is more important than the fear that we're feeling. That's it, that's the 'magic pill'. We plant in our minds that no matter how much we fear something, we know that something else is more important than that fear and we act despite it.

The great ones aren't where they are because they found a way to stop fearing rejection. The great ones are where they are because they realized that no matter what they do they're going to continue to fear rejection. That thought right there should free us from our thoughts of worry about the fear that we feel. We don't have to worry about being rejected because WE WILL be rejected. We don't have to worry about failing because WE WILL fail. It's all a part of the process. That's not meant to provide a gloomy look at our career in sales but instead to show a different and better way to view the fear that has been taking us over for so long.

Want a paradigm shift when it comes to the fear we feel for rejection? Start taking steps to seek out rejection in your daily life. Start asking people things that are a little out of the ordinary. Ask a few people close to you if they'd like to go on a trip to Africa with you (It obviously doesn't have to be Africa but pick some type of spontaneous destination). Tell them a little about what you'd like to do, like go on a safari or visit a tribe. Most of them are likely to look at you like you're crazy or assume you're just joking around but I'd bet if you asked 35-40 people that you know you'd find 5-6 people or more that would at least be intrigued by the idea of doing it if they knew you were serious. That's oddly similar to your sales ratio isn't it? Hmmmm...

I'm certainly not telling you that we're going to start feeling so comfortable with rejection that we will no longer ever have fear again. That's not going to be the case, but realizing that rejection is going to be a part of our lives no matter what we do may set us up to have a different outlook on what it means in our career.

Reason #2

You SUCK Because You Make Excuses, Lots of Them

If I was to ask you right now what is holding you back from being the best salesman in your company, what would you say? Let's make this an exercise. Seriously, grab a notepad or even a little sticky note and write down the ten reasons why you aren't the best salesman in your company. It shouldn't take you longer than a minute or two so go for it...

If you didn't do that tiny exercise then I hate to say this but you're probably the guy that just reads and reads on how to become a better salesman yet never actually implements anything effectively because you're constantly searching for some magic potion that's easily usable. If that one hit home a little bit and you still haven't completed the exercise please do so now. Believe me, doing this has the opportunity to be a huge step in taking your career and life to a whole new level.

Now that we have those written down, or we're at

least thinking about them in our heads, we can start to break them down to better understand what we can do about them. Here's what the beginning my list would've looked like when I first started in my sales career:

1. My territory is different than everyone else's and/or people are different

2. The economy isn't very good right now, people don't have the money to buy

3. There aren't enough potential clients in my area

4. I don't have time to do all the things I'm being asked to do

I could go on and on about different things that I was telling myself as to why I wasn't the best salesman in my company and why I felt that I never could be the best. We all do that at certain times in our career because for some reason we think we're unique. Well folks, we're not unique. None of us are. We all have the same tools given to us by our companies to get the job done.

Let's break down my excuses so we can better understand why they aren't valid in any of our situations:

1. My territory is different than everyone else's and/or the people are different

Your territory is no different than anyone else's. Maybe your territory is a little more difficult than others to work in and continually develop business in but obviously the company would not put you in a position where they would expect you to fail. We need to man up and get the job done. We need to prove to both the company and to ourselves that we can make it through challenging situations, even if it may be a little bit tougher for us than others.

2. The economy isn't very good right now, people don't have the money to buy

This is an automatic excuse for anybody in sales because many potential clients will actually say this to you as a reason they can't buy right now. We need to realize that while this may be a valid excuse for some businesses to not partner with us it's not an excuse for us to not do what we need to do. Sure, a struggling economy makes it tougher for us to sell at a high level but it certainly doesn't mean we can't sell. Our closing ratio may go down into the 10% range or lower and we may need to seek out more potential clients but there will always be people in a position to buy what we're selling.

3. There aren't enough potential clients in my area

This was my favorite when I was in what I call my 'excuse era'. I was absolutely convinced that there weren't enough people in my territory that were potential prospects. In the end it was all a lie and there were plenty of prospects in my area, just as there are in yours. Like I said, it's going to be harder for some people than others but in the end it's all about making the decision that no matter how hard it is we're going to make it. Struggles are going to come our way, there's no doubt about that. In the end we need to realize that we all have the opportunity to succeed in our areas, no matter how gloomy it may at first seem.

4. I don't have time to do all the things I'm being asked to do

A lot of times people get into sales because of the flexibility that it provides. If you're an outside sales representative than you're probably setting your own schedule as it pertains to your life. I'm amazed at the amount of us that make excuses about the limited amount of time we have to give to our careers simply because of our kids or families. Like I said, we're not unique. We're not the only person out there that has kids, a family, and other responsibilities to go with our careers. Using our kids as scapegoats for the lack of success in our careers is absolutely ludicrous. If this is your excuse then here's another little exercise:

Sit your kids down on the couch and let them know that you need to speak with them about something. Now tell them that it's their fault that you can't be successful in your career and that they're holding you back from reaching your potential.

That sounds absolutely ridiculous right? Yep, well so is that excuse…We'll get back to that list you just made in a minute. First I want to talk about another process of excuse making that is holding many people back from any chance at success in their sales career.

While that overview provides an outlook on some of the excuses that we make about why we can't be successful in our careers, there's another layer to excuses that sets many people up for failure from the very beginning. The type - people that make excuses and/or blame others for why they didn't do something right.

Let me give you this scenario:

Joe is 16 years old, playing in his high school's state championship baseball game. His team is down one run with guys on second and third and two outs. It's the last chance for his team, a base hit wins it while an out obviously ends it.

First pitch is a ball. Next pitch is a called high strike and he wheels around and gives the umpire an intense glare because he didn't feel it was anywhere near a strike. Counts at 1-1 and he's already got it in his head that he was cheated of that strike. The at-bat goes on and the counts now at 3-2. Here's where things get dicey. The next pitch is a fastball right on the outside corner and Joe takes it. Called strike three, game over, Joe blew it. Joe immediately begins screaming at the umpire after the called strike three while the other team celebrates their win.

In this example Joe had already had it in his mind that he had a scapegoat for not succeeding. If he didn't come through he could just blame the umpire and everyone else would do the same. So, instead of fighting through the bad call and actually trying to succeed, Joe already had pre-determined that he had an excuse and someone to blame for why he failed.

There are a good amount of people in this world that live their lives that way. Instead of 'failing', they set themselves up so that it can't possibly be their fault if they fail. They have a built in excuse for why they are going to fail before they even fail. There's no possible way to ever be successful using this mentality because you'll never have the belief necessary to make things happen.

If you want something to happen in your life, if you want to be successful, then YOU need to be the one to make that happen. It's not your families fault or your bosses fault or your co-workers fault. It's your fault. Stop counting on other people to get things done for you and make it happen for yourself. Start taking accountability for your own life and realize that nobody determines your fate but you.

Now if you still have that list with your excuses on it I want you to immediately rip it up into as many little pieces as you can and throw it away. That's the last time you are going to use excuses for why you aren't where you want to be in your career. There's no longer anyone to blame but ourselves for why we aren't the best salesperson in our company.

The only way to get rid of excuses in your life and in your career is to stop making them. Think of how much our lives would improve if we simply rid ourselves of all excuses and found a way to get things done. What do you think you would be able to accomplish in the next week, month, year and beyond if you made a commitment to stop making excuses and go after what you want?

Make a commitment to yourself that every time an excuse pops into your head about why you can't do something that you will immediately replace that thought with, 'Doesn't matter, I'm going to do it anyhow.' The amount that this change in perception will improve your life and career is drastic. Implement a no excuse mentality into your own life and watch the influence that it will have on your life and career.

Reason #3

You SUCK Because You're Not Self-Disciplined Enough

If I had to pick the number one reason that most sales professionals are not successful it would undoubtedly be that they are not self-disciplined. There are plenty of people that have what it takes to go out and sell at a 10-20% clip, they just don't have the discipline to consistently do it over the long term.

How do we define self-discipline? The Webster definition goes a little something like this, 'The ability to make yourself do things that should be done'.

Self-discipline means not getting caught up in the emotions of our daily lives. So our first appointment of the day ended with an angry potential client telling us that our prices are too high and that nobody is ever going to buy what we have for that price. We start thinking about what they said and we start to question everything that comes with our job. The price, the quality of the product or service, the type of salespeople that we are. We start to question it all. What we need to realize is that this potential customer said this because we didn't present the type of value that we needed to present in order for them to understand that what we are offering really is worth that price.

We can't get caught up in the opinions of people who know little to nothing about our products or services and what they can provide for them. If they think that our prices are entirely too high and that nobody in our area is ever going to pay that price then we must have done a horrible job at building value for the product or service that we're selling. It was our fault and we need to learn from it and move on.

Our jobs as sales professionals is to raise the value of our product or service to the point where the person sitting across from us pictures a price for our product or service that is much lower than what our prices actually are. If our product or service costs $1,000, we need to build the price in their heads to be somewhere around the $1,500-$2,000 range. Anyhow, defining our jobs is another subject for another day.

This is about having the self-discipline to help us succeed over the long term. Leave the emotions out of your career. Take the hit, brush it off, and continue doing what you need to do. If somebody feeds us a bunch of BS about how our product or service is far too expensive then we need to have the self-discipline to understand that we didn't do a good job presenting what we needed to present. It was our fault, we'll learn from it, and we'll move on to the next one unhindered by the comments of the previous appointment.

The first part of this chapter talked about having the self-discipline to not let emotions get the best of us and to continue doing what we need to do regardless of the opinions of others. The second part of this chapter is going to talk about the action plans that we need to create in order to become self-disciplined sales professionals.

Many of us get into the field of sales because of the flexibility that it provides in our daily lives. Outside sales representatives usually have the opportunity to create their own schedule as it relates to their outside lives. The problem here, however, is that many times this flexibility becomes a curse because of a lack of self-discipline. Because of this flexibility we fall into a trap where we feel as if we have the opportunity to work less hours than the normal 40 hour work week and still make a comfortable living. While that may be true for many of us, most of us can't afford the luxury of working only 4-5 hours a day and make a substantial income from it.

We've got to have the self-discipline to follow through on what we have planned to do. Find out your numbers, write them down, and map out a plan for how you are going to follow through with those numbers. This is absolutely essential for us to succeed as sales professionals. We are set up for failure from the beginning if we ignore the fact that we need to have a plan that we follow through with every single day and every single week.

Whatever your schedule is, map it out for the next quarter. I like to work in quarters because most companies look over their numbers on a quarterly basis and you may even be in a position where you receive quarterly bonuses for certain levels of production. Mapping out our plans on a quarterly basis allows us the opportunity to have some longevity to our plans but not be so long that a faulty plan keeps us from having a good year.

If we have the self-discipline to follow the numbers, the results will come through accordingly. Having our numbers mapped out and having a plan will make us feel much more comfortable with ourselves. Maybe your closing ratio will end up being 15% or maybe you've improved enough that it'll be 30% this quarter. One of my favorite practices is to figure out my closing percentage over the past year, lower it by 5% and then map out the numbers that I need to achieve my goals from that. This gives me some leeway if my closing percentage doesn't end up being the usual and also means that if my closing percentage stays the same or even improves whatsoever that I'll have an outstanding quarter.

While we want to know our numbers prior to making our quarterly plan, over the course of the quarter don't focus on your numbers whatsoever. Keep track of them but don't count them up. It'll only put you in a situation where emotions will come through and try to convince you that what you're doing is not going to be successful. Make a plan for the quarter and stick to it, whether it seems to be working or not. At the end of the quarter you can evaluate your plan and see what you can change to make things better. Changing your plan mid quarter will only make you lose belief in the path that you're going down. Make the plan, believe in it, and stick to it.

You can't just make a plan and watch it go to waste. You've got to make the commitment and have the self-discipline to stick to the plan. Action is the only thing that is going to make your plan become a reality. It's an absolute must that you have an action plan for your daily life. If you have kids to take care of and you have to take them to school and pick them up, stop using that as an excuse and map out the time that you're going to work. If your schedule has to be 9:00-2:30, stick to that and make sure you do everything in your power to have everything you need to have ready to go when that time comes. Our planned schedules should not be a time when we are making plans for what we are going to do during our day; that needs to be mapped out well beforehand.

Many successful sales professionals make an effort to plan out their week on the Friday of the week before. Others map out a time period over the weekend where they make their weekly plans.

Figure out a time that works for you to map out your upcoming week. You want to be in a situation every week where when Monday comes you're ready to go. There's no thinking about what you need to do and there's no doubt about how you're going to do it. Planning time should be over, it's time to get down to business and make some sales. If you need to make cold calls then you should be mapping out who you're going to call before going into the week. There should be absolutely no doubt about what you're going to be doing for the week.

The best salespeople are also the most consistent salespeople. They know what they want and they know what they need to get there. They know their numbers and they map out exactly how many cold calls, how many appointments they need to go on, and how many hours they need to work in order to reach their goals. Focus on the things that you can control. Know how many calls you have to make to set an appointment. Know how many appointments you need to make a sale. Look at the things that you can control and focus on those things explicitly. Everything else is completely irrelevant.

Even the most self-disciplined people in the world

can fall apart when they don't put themselves in a position to succeed. You've got to set yourself up so that you know where you want to be and find a way to take yourself there.

Here's an overview of the steps you need to take to force yourself into a self-disciplined mindset:

1. **Find out your numbers**

- Figure out how many calls it takes to set an appointment, how many app. to make a sale, etc.

2. **Make a quarterly plan**

- Once you have those numbers devise a plan where you lower your closing percentage by 5% and map out what you need to do to reach your sales goals at that percentage

- Believe in this plan and stick to it throughout the quarter no matter how bad you may struggle

3. **Make a weekly plan**

- Prior to every week throughout the quarter figure out exactly what you're going to be doing during your scheduled work time (Friday night or sometime over weekend)

- Planning should NEVER be done during your planned work period

4. Get rid of all excuses

- When you make your plans there should be absolutely no excuses for not fulfilling what you set out to do

- Your car broke down? Find a way to complete your plans anyhow...

- Your kids got sick? Find a way to work through it...

- Your great aunt passed away? FIND A WAY!

Reason #4

You SUCK Because You're Weird (Yeah, You Heard Me!)

Alright people, this is where things start to get real. This chapter is going to pinpoint why you being a weirdo is what's holding you back from being a solid sales professional.

A lot of times you'll hear people say that salesmen have to be a different breed of person. That's undoubtedly true to a certain degree but we must also realize that 'different breed' does not mean being weird.

The reason many of us struggle with selling early in our careers is because we're so darn weird. People don't like to be put in awkward situations so they're automatically going to go a flight mentality if they run into a guy that they deem weird, especially when he's trying to sell them something. I used to be a weird salesman too. Really, really weird.

I remember the first cold call I ever made in my

sales career was to a guy named Jim. I was selling advertising for a local print magazine company and gave Jim a ring. After getting past the gatekeeper, Jim answers the phone, *'This is Jim, what can I do for you?'* I immediately said back to him with a ridiculously giddy voice, *'Hey Jim, my name's Jim too! Can you believe that!,'* and then just sat there in silence.

What in the hell was I even saying?!? What a freakin' weirdo I was...

After sitting there in silence for an excessively long five seconds Jim said back to me, *'Yeahhhh, alright, what can I do for you?'* As I started on my spiel for what I was selling I heard the phone click in the most subtle way possible. Jim hung up on me because I was a weird guy trying to sell him something. I'm kind of glad it happened on my very first call because from then on it made me squeamish to even think about how weird I was to Jim.

That scenario may not seem like that big of a deal to you and you may even be thinking that this is normal in your own sales career. Well good, we found out that you're weird as well! We're going to fix that right now.

Be yourself.

Now let's dive into what I mean by weird a little more. Being weird means doing or saying things that just simply aren't normal for you. Weird is completely different from being unique so let's be sure not to confuse the two of them. Being unique is something that can greatly benefit you in your sales career because you'll be doing things that most salespeople don't do and you'll have the opportunity to separate yourself from the salesman persona. Weird salesmen are everywhere, unique salesmen are few and far between.

Stop trying to mold yourself into this generic proper salesman role that so many people like to present. This concept that every salesman should be wearing a suit and tie and constantly be creating generic rapport is ridiculous. There is no proper salesman role. People don't enjoy talking to superficial people. Think of your own life and the friends that you have in it. Do you enjoy people that you immediately label as salesman? Do you involve people in your life that are superficial or that you can clearly see put on a second persona when they speak to you? People don't like people that are weird or superficial because they don't relate to them and they definitely don't trust them.

People buy from people they like. If you've read any type of book or article on sales you probably are already aware of that. They don't like to talk to a bunch of generic people that are clearly acting in order to get something from them. It's easier than you may think to find out if someone has an ulterior motive for being excessively nice or friendly. These people aren't looking for fake and you're certainly not the first generic salesman to present a bunch of self-serving BS to them. They want someone that's real, someone that they can trust. I mean seriously can you not understand how incredibly stupid you sound when you're just spitting out a bunch of words that you memorized. Remember that awful speech your best friend made in that one class in high school? Yea, that sounds like you during your presentation.

Being fake presents an environment where it is almost impossible for a potential customer or client to buy something from you. Nobody is ever going to buy something off of someone they don't trust. This comes from years of people being screwed over by untrustworthy salesmen who threw in multiple curveballs with hidden fees or expenses that were never presented to the person before the agreement. Be truthful and real to your potential clients and they will respect you greatly for it.

People either love or hate people that are upfront and real with them. In sales we should look at this as a positive because there's no middle ground to sort through. Your sales presentation will be about creating truth, informing, and asking relevant questions to determine what the best plan of action is for the customer. There won't be any middle ground about whether they like you or don't like you and whether they like the product or service or not. When you're upfront with other people they in turn are usually upfront right back to you. They'll be real with you and not take you through the ringer that some people call the 'sales cycle'. So many people waste so much darn time on a client that just didn't have the guts to say no because they know all it will result in is a bunch of ready-made answers to their objection.

Some people just don't have the guts to simply say no so they instead come up with a bunch of excuses for why they can't sign up today or why they have to ask a few other people if this is a good idea. Most of the time it's just a generic response to someone they don't trust so they don't have to say no to them. Instead of saying no they tell you to call back in a few days and then end up telling you that it 'isn't in their budget' or 'it isn't a good fit for them right now'...Or they tell you to come back in a week or two and set up a second appointment. If you've been in sales for an extended period of time you probably already realize that this rarely ever results in a sale. I'm sure there are quite a few of you saying that this happens all the time to you and you get a lot of sales from situations where the potential customer or client says they'll call you back.

Be real with people and they'll be real with you in return. Ask up front questions and expect upfront answers. Have a conversation with them instead of talking a bunch of BS to them. There will definitely be a few people that won't appreciate the upfront personality but know that there will be plenty more that will appreciate it. Not everybody is going to buy from you in the first place and it'll be obvious whether someone appreciates you being up front and forward with them. If they don't appreciate it, they probably won't buy, but at least you can confirm that right off the bat and won't have to turn into a stalker who calls them every couple days to ask if they're interested. If they do appreciate your forwardness, there's a much better chance they will buy. Nobody wants to waste time and it's better for everybody if everything's out on the table the first time you meet with somebody. Stop wasting so much time and get things out on the table from the very beginning. This also creates a vibe of confidence that will shine as you run through your presentations.

The last thing you need to do in order to stop being so weird is to stop begging. Begging is incredibly unattractive. Think of how unattractive it has been in the past when one of your former girlfriends or boyfriends has begged for you to come back into their lives. Begging has the opposite effect of its intentions. It creates a situation where the person that is being begged to just wants to completely disassociate themselves from the situation. Don't go in there like some homeless person that needs this sale to survive. If you don't make the sale, you'll still live and you'll learn from it.

Here's an overview of what your mindset should be while speaking to a potential client or customer to ensure that you're not being one of those freakin' weirdo salespeople that engulf the profession:

1. **Be thoroughly engaged and interested in what your potential customer or client's wants and needs are**

- DON'T be fake about it

- Authentically care about them and what they want or need

2. **Present in a way that is straightforward, engaging, and efficient**

    - Don't be a robot and don't say generic things

    - Have a conversation and consistently engage them throughout the presentation

    - Shut up and let them talk by asking relevant questions about their needs (Split should be around 60% you talking, 40% them talking)

3. Create push away, just not too much

- DON'T beg them to buy from you

- Be in control of the process and let them know that if what you have isn't a good fit for them then that's fine

Combining all of these mindsets is going to take time and each one of them could easily have its own book on the topic. Slowly working these mindsets into your presentation is going to make both you and the person you're presenting to enjoy a much more comfortable and natural experience. Stop being so stinking weird watch what inserting these mindsets can do for your sales career!

Reason #5

You SUCK Because You Haven't Failed Enough!

This is where things really start to get interesting and you start to question everything. I'm here to tell you that you suck at sales because you've never been a failure. You've had things handed to you so much throughout your life that you never had the luxury of experiencing immense and constant failure. Yea, you read that right, the luxury of constant failure.

See, when you fail, things happen. Emotions come bounding through your body and doubt begins to creep into your mind about whether you can do something. You feel down, sad, and upset and you feel like all your energy has been snapped out of you. But then something else happens. You realize that you'll still live through the failure. You realize that at the end of the day your failure wasn't really as big of a deal as you made it out to be. You learn from it and realize that your failures help you build emotional stability and help you grow in your career.

You can sit around and read all the sales books there is to offer but if you don't make a commitment to failure you'll never be successful. I'm telling you that you've literally got to make a commitment to failing. You've got to say to yourself that I'm going to go through whatever I need to go through and I'm going to fail as many times as it takes for me to be successful.

Winston Churchill once said, 'Success consists of going from failure to failure without loss of enthusiasm.' You've got to be aware that failure is a part of the process of becoming successful and that there is absolutely no way to avoid it if you are truly going to reach the top. Understanding this vital fact will allow you to view the process of failure in a new and positive light. When you understand that failure is necessary you'll start to see yourself learning and growing through the failure process. You'll start to improve your abilities and see that being great at something like sales is impossible without failing thousands of times throughout the process.

People that are successful haven't been successful for the entirety of their lives. If they tell you they've never failed they're both lying and also not anywhere near as successful as they claim to be. Study the most successful people that this world's ever seen and you'll see that they are all intensely humble. They've been through everything there is to go through and they've been beaten down and thrown around by everybody and anybody.

Failure is an inevitable part of the process of being successful in our business. You're going to have times where you go two or three weeks without selling a thing. There's a good chance, depending on what type of sales you're in, you might even go two or three months without a sale at some point in your career.

These struggles make us feel like sales isn't for us. We feel like giving up. The thing that we don't usually understand however is that all of the greats have had those same struggles throughout their lives. They had the same thoughts and struggles that you're experiencing or that you've been experiencing up to this point.

Now that we have a better understanding of the necessity of failure in order to be successful, let's take a look at a type of failure that is not going to help you learn and grow.

Let's go back to our scenario with Joe playing baseball:

Joe is 16 years old, playing in his high school's state championship baseball game. His team is down one run with guys on second and third and two outs. It's the last chance for his team, a base hit wins it while an out obviously ends it.

First pitch is a ball. Next pitch is a called high strike and he wheels around and gives the umpire an intense glare because he didn't feel it was anywhere near a strike. Counts at 1-1 and he's already got it in his head that he was cheated of that strike. The at-bat goes on and the counts now at 3-2. Here's where things get dicey. The next pitch is a fastball right on the outside corner and Joe takes it. Called strike three, game over, Joe blew it. Joe immediately begins screaming at the umpire after the called strike three while the other team celebrates their win.

As I mentioned before there are a good amount of people in this world that live their lives that way. Instead of 'failing', they set themselves up so that it can't possibly be their fault if they fail. This gets in the way of your ability to learn from failure because all you're doing is making an excuse for why the failure occurred. You come to the conclusion that any failure couldn't possibly be your fault and you search for someone or something that you can blame for the mishap.

This is where accountability needs to come in. You need to realize that if you fail, it's your fault. It was up to you to succeed and you failed. The important thing to understand here though is that your failure wasn't that big of a deal. It's all a process. You need to fail in order to get where you want to be. Stop viewing failure as something that you couldn't possibly accept for yourself. When it happens, accept it, take the blame and move on.

Yes I know, some of you know a guy in your company that is selling at a 60% clip. Yep I heard the same thing you did on the conference call about how Joe Schmo is selling at a 65% clip for the year and already met his quota three months in. He's like some type of guru that can sell everything and anything. You want to know what you have to do to get on his level. Well, what Joe didn't tell you is that he used to be a failure. He used to sell at a

5% clip and had nights where he thought about giving up on sales.

You've absolutely got to be a failure before you can get anywhere in your life. Many of the greatest businessmen that we know today were once broke and homeless. John Paul DeJoria was homeless and had $700 to his name when he started what turned into a multi-billion dollar hair care company. Larry Ellison dropped out of college and worked odd jobs for eight years before starting Oracle, a software development company. Ellison and DeJoria both now have a net-worth over $15 billion. The guy's who made the world famous Angry Birds game had made over 50 different games that had failed miserably before finally having their big breakthrough. There are thousands of stories just like these about business owners that made it after failing over and over again throughout their lives.

How doesn't that inspire you? These guys didn't have anything special about them that led them to where they are. They were self-disciplined, hard working, and self-motivated. They knew what they were going to do and they went after it. That's exactly what you need to do. Stop viewing failure as something that is ruining your life and start viewing it as the thing that is going to get you where you want to be in your career.

You SUCK Because You Don't Care About What You're Selling

If you don't care about what you're selling then it's going to show, and it's going to show a lot. I honestly have no idea how people even do this. How in the world do you sell something that you don't care about? It doesn't make any sense. My guess is that if you're selling something you don't care about then you also hate your job. Why in the world would you do or sell something that you hate? It seriously, legitimately, doesn't make one bit of sense to me.

If you don't have a purpose for why you're doing something, if you don't have a profound interest in what your product or service is doing for the consumer, then you're going to be absolutely awful at your job. Even worse, you're going to hate getting up for work every day. It's essential that you find your purpose for why you're selling what you're selling. Find out why you care about what you're selling and what it does to improve the lives of the consumer.

Are you selling a service that is going to help business owners increase their sales? Then you're helping business owners achieve their dreams. Are you selling insurance so families aren't hit with unforeseen expenses that could ruin their financial lives? Then you're helping families have a more comfortable and enjoyable life. What you are selling isn't the issue here. Whether what you're selling means anything to you is the issue.

So what do you do if you're not passionate about what you're selling? That's easy, you quit. If you don't enjoy what you sell, quit and find something that you actually care about.

What?!? You can't just go and quit your job and find a new one though right? Wrong. Anyone worth their weight in anything can go find another job that they enjoy and can therefore be much better at. There are plenty of jobs out there for salesmen, it's the one job that will always have a multitude of opportunities in a capitalistic society. People will always need to sell their products, and there will always be a market for certain products no matter what the economic situation may be.

Stop feeling as if you're tied to your current position simply because it's something you've become comfortable doing. Getting in a comfort zone is a dangerous place to be in because it provides little room for growth. You should be consistently seeking out opportunities to grow as a person and as a professional. Attaching yourself to a company or product that you don't believe in is going to provide very little growth for your life. This is your life we're talking about here. You only get one of them. Why spend it selling something you don't believe in?

If you can't find it in yourself to have at least a little bit of passion about what you're selling then you're in the wrong business. Regret is a terrible thing. Don't be that guy that doesn't realize until he's 50 years old that he's hated his job for the past 20 years and can't wait to retire. So many people live their lives in a race to retire. That's got to be absolutely miserable. Sure, everybody needs to earn a living and support their families, but there is absolutely no reason to be miserable in your job for a good portion of your life.

I know this chapter seems a bit dramatic. The comfort zone that you're in right now would never allow you to step out and try a new experience. You can't afford to leave your current job because you need the immediate paychecks to support your family. Leaving your current position would mean trying something new and experiencing a great deal of discomfort for the time that you are uncertain about your new job. Believe me, I get it, I've been there. But we can go through a more comfortable process to determine whether the job we have is something we want to continue down:

1. Figure out why you're selling what you're selling

- Try to come to a conclusion in which you realize that what you're selling provides value to other people's lives

2. Take a good hard look at your job and ask yourself if you're passionate about it or if you could develop passion it for it by viewing it in a different light

- *If you can't come to a sufficient conclusion on these two things then you need to get out of your current situation. Your career literally depends on it…

Ok, but you can't actually just up and quit your job because you really do have to support your family and you can't afford the lapse in paychecks. Well then start seeking out other opportunities while you're working. Research some things at night that interest you that you could be passionate about. Good sales professionals are always going to be in high demand. Be confident in your abilities and go out and find something that you will enjoy selling. Don't be that guy rushing through life trying to get to retirement as fast as possible. Enjoy what you do and reap the rewards that come with it.

Reason #7

You SUCK Because You Haven't Made the Decision to Become the Absolute BEST

As a high school athletics coach, it drives me absolutely bonkers when I see kids show up and not want to go all out with what they do. They make the decision to show up every single day and spend a great deal of their lives at practice and doing workouts, yet they also seem to make the decision to be mediocre. Too many of us do the exact same thing within our sales careers.

Why would you ever want to make the decision to be mediocre? If you're going to be here, if you've already made the decision that this is going to be your job and that you're going to grow within this career then why in the world would you plan on being mediocre? Why would you mold your career around just showing up and not being exceptional?

It's an absolutely ridiculous concept to me. Think of all the perks that come with being great. The financial incentives, the recognition, the opportunity for promotion. You've already made the decision to show up, why not also make the decision to be great at what you do.

Now think of all the things that come with being mediocre or below average. Financial trouble, possible demotions or remaining stagnant with no growth, feeling that you're alone in the company and that everybody is doing better than you. There are all types of negative consequences that come with being mediocre and/or below average while making the decision to be the best provides enormous rewards.

Every single person that has the ability to get the job in the first place also has the ability to be the best. The top people in your company aren't special. They don't have any kind of special talents that make them who they are. One thing they did do however is make the decision to be the best and they followed through and made it happen. They turned their career into a competition. They made it almost like a game, a game that they could enjoy.

You can't be the best without first making the decision that you want to be the best. Make that decision right now and educate yourself on what the best people in your company are doing. What time do they get up? How many appointments do they do a week? How many phone calls do they make a week? You don't have to mirror what you do after them but pick out what you think is most important and make an effort to do that. Once you get to their level you can begin to experiment a little more with what you think can take you to whole new levels.

Being great involves developing a system for improving yourself on a regular basis. When you're at work be at work and when you're at home or doing something else be there. There's no reason to mix the two.

I want to ask you a very serious question and I want you to answer it as honestly as possible. You don't have to share your answer with anybody but I want you to seriously consider your answer and see what you can do about it.

What is the point of being average? What is the point of dedicating your life to something that you don't enjoy. Statistics show that most people spend 50% of their waking hours on their careers. If you're spending it being average then wouldn't you look at it as time wasted. We don't have a whole lot of time on this beautiful earth so why not do everything we can to make the best of it while we're here. Don't waste 50% of your life half-assing something. If you're going to do it, if you've made the decision that sales will be your career and that you honestly enjoy the sales process then make the decision to do it to the best of your ability. There's no reason not to.

There's no reason to wake up every day not knowing where you're going or how you're going to get there. Make the decision to be the best, figure out what you need to do to get there and then take the action to get there. You have the opportunity to do it. There's nothing holding you back from being the best besides beliefs that have been drilled into you since you were a youngster. The opportunity is there, but it's up to you. It's up to you to make your career what you want it to be. No one else is in charge of your life and the way you live it. It's all on you.

Most people live in a world where they honestly believe that outside circumstances need to come together and the perfect storm needs to be created in order for them to be great or in order for them to be the best. These people blame others for their struggles and constantly make excuses for why they aren't where they want to be. You can't really blame people for this type of thinking, especially since it's much easier to do this than to buckle up and realize that your life is in your own hands. It's hard to be great, it's hard to be the best. The people who are the best, the greats in the business, are people who made the decision to do things that everybody else chose not to do. They made the decision to do the things that they knew they needed to do, even when they didn't feel like doing it. They found something bigger than themselves to attach to and made the place where they're going far more important than the struggles that they would have to go through to get there.

The life that you have the potential to live, the career that you have the potential to have, is incredible. If you really knew what you were capable of it would absolutely blow your mind. You'd want to stand up and say, *'Wow, I am f'in great.'* Some people never find out the potential that is within them. They surround themselves with people that float through life thinking that being average is a part of life. That some people are born with things that they weren't born with, that they don't have what it takes to be in a position to be the best of the best.

It's all a lie. You have the opportunity to be the best, you just have to be willing to make the decision that you're going to be the best. You have to make the decision that you're going to do what it takes to be the best and that no struggles or hardships are going to get in your way. You're not going to be dominated by the emotions and struggles that you're going to have to fight through in order to be the best.

That guy that says he's never struggled or never been put through the ringer. That guy that says he was always a natural at what he did and never struggled or failed along the way. He's a liar. The great ones have all struggled just like you're struggling right now. They just knew that jumping through the hoops that you're jumping through now were necessary in order to be the best. They kept fighting and fighting because they knew exactly where they were going.

So what about you? What's holding you back from being the best? Is it your beliefs? Is it that you've been making too many excuses or blaming others? Is it because you don't do things when you don't feel like doing them? Whatever your reason it's your responsibility to figure it out and make the necessary changes to improve yourself. Make the decision to go beyond where you've ever reached before and make the decision that you, that person reading this right this very second, is going to be the best salesman that your company has to offer. Do it. You've got everything to gain and absolutely nothing to lose.

Final Words

It's Time To Get Out There And Make Something Happen!

I want to thank you and congratulate you for transiting my lines from start to finish. I'm fully aware that the philosophy here presented is, at times, difficult to assimilate. We're used to something else. We're accustomed to other time requirements, demands, and mental boundaries. But that's precisely the point.

It's about being different. Because by definition, being successful means being different. It involves thinking with your own mind, no matter how loud outside voices yell. It implies trusting fully in your own capabilities, and loving yourself so much that you don't even conceive accepting a life that doesn't represent and materialize all the energy and creative power you possess. It means pushing forward through the wall of rejection over and over again until the big doors finally open.

I'm convinced that the hunger, ambition, and desire to improve that lies within you will elevate you to the order of the extraordinary. You were born to make a difference in the world. And that difference will be the one you decide to make.

I must admit I'm ecstatic to know there are people fighting tirelessly for what they want. So I sincerely dedicate you my deepest respect, and I encourage you to continue with a firm and decisive step on the path we've passionately chosen to walkthrough.

And why not? Maybe we'll meet at some point down the way.

Until then,

William Wyatt

Preview of "Alpha Male: Stop Being a P#ssy, Become an Alpha Male - The Ultimate Guide to Attract Women & Achieve Massive Success In Life"

Introduction

Are You Ready to Go Alpha?

Where is your life at right now? Are you where you want to be? Are you an alpha male? Do women easily come to you because of the many different traits that you easily portray? Do you have an aura about you that forces people to flock towards you?

Are you walking around blaming others for your problems and making excuses for why you aren't where you want to be? Seriously, take a second and think about the amount of occasions that you've made excuses for certain problems in your life. Times that you've blamed others for misfortunes that in the end were your fault.

Don't lie to yourself here. Don't be that douche bag with the oversized ego that can't take the time to step back and understand that there are opportunities out there to improve his standing in this world. Maybe you're in a position right now where you're trying to convince yourself that you're moving in the right direction and yet you can't seem to make the changes necessary. You're trying to find a way to become sought out by women. You're trying to find a way to overcome the constant struggles and stress of your day to day life.

Are you this guy?

This book has the opportunity to change all these things. This book has the opportunity to open up your mind to the things that you're currently missing in your life. This book has the opportunity to transform you and help you develop a life that will force women to flock to you.

This may come across a bit on the arrogant side to some, but just realize that it's for your own good. You need this right now. You need someone that isn't going to listen to your excuses and isn't going to allow you to walk through life like some scared teen that can't even look his crush in the eye. You're going to be insulted at times and you're going to feel like this alpha male thing isn't quite for you. But it is. You have an opportunity here to change your life.

It's time, boys. It's time to make sure that that's the last time anyone calls you a boy. It's time to get it done. It's time to become that male figure that everyone else looks up to. It's time to sit back, throw the excuses and ego out the window, and get ready to become an alpha male.

Let's f**kin do this...

Chapter #1

Defining an Alpha Male - What He Is, What He Isn't

So, what's the definition of an alpha male? Well, our trusted friend Webster's dictionary defines an alpha male as the most dominant, powerful, assertive man in a particular group. That's what we're going for here.

While that may be the beginning of what we perceive as an alpha male, the train certainly doesn't stop there. Let's dive a little further into what being an alpha male really means...

An alpha male is a confident man who is deeply passionate about his life. An alpha male is composed and driven, always knowing what he wants and what he needs to do to get it. An alpha male is a man of deep morals and values who is perceived by others to be incredibly trustworthy. An alpha male is a natural conversationalist and leader, he knows how to create conversation and sustain it in a comfortable and intriguing way. An alpha male is physically fit and understands the value of a healthy lifestyle throughout their lives. An alpha male consistently demonstrates strength and dominance, although they stray far away from flaunting it. They know the line between arrogance and confidence and they make sure to walk that line in a meticulous way on a daily basis.

An alpha male is not a bully and does not boss others around. He understands that being a leader involves leading by example and has nothing to do with telling others what to do. He doesn't look down or talk down on others but instead focuses on lifting people up and inspiring them.

An alpha male is not someone who is afraid of fear. He understands that fear is a part of life and that it is nothing more than a necessary hurdle on the way to a planned end.

An alpha male does not talk himself up or make attempts to prove himself but is instead talked up by others because of the way he lives his life and the morals and values that he holds true.

So you're thinking right now, 'Wow, this alpha male guy seems like the f**kin man!' You're probably also thinking that you yourself could never achieve a level quite like the stature of a true alpha male.

Every single male on this earth has the ability to

create a life for themselves that revolves around being an alpha male. A life that's void of worry and panic, but full of confidence and poise. A life that you're passionate about and a view of the world where you know that you can go after and achieve anything that you desire.

Some people float through life feeling sorry for themselves and have this overwhelming sense that they have no control of where they are going or how they are getting there. They feel as if they're constantly in a state of confusion and can never really find out what they want out of life or how they're going to get there.

That's not the life of an alpha male. An alpha male knows what he wants and he goes after it relentlessly. He awakens every single day, not because his alarm clock went off, but because he is so courageously passionate about the day ahead of him and the opportunities at his disposal. He knows that the only way to achieve success is to work, and work damn hard. He's not scared to go out of his comfort zone and what others see as difficult and struggle he sees as an opportunity to go above the norm. He views failure as nothing more than a learning experience and stepping stone on the path he has designed for his life.

He's a boss and he knows it -the Rick Ross version, not the McDonald's manager version- and so does everyone else. There is absolutely no doubt when he walks in a room that he is in charge. He has an aura about him that leaves an impression that he may be the next coming of Jesus Christ.

Alright, so now we're getting a little out of hand. At least you get the idea by now. This man has his shit together and everybody knows it. He is completely in control of his day and doesn't let outside circumstances dictate the way that he lives his life. Little things don't bug him as he knows, at the end of the day, life will go on in a magnificent way.

He is constantly in control of his thoughts and emotions and doesn't let insignificant things take control over his daily life. His tire just blew out on the way to work? He doesn't give a shit. He gets out of his car, puts the spare tire on, and goes to work. He doesn't spend the day bitching about what happened to his car and has no interest in having others feel sorry for him because of it.

An alpha male has an intense sense of pride about getting things done. He understands that his word should be guarded at all costs. When he says something is going to get done, it gets done. He avoids excuses at all costs and always finds a way to get it done, no matter what difficulties he faces in the process.

Ever wonder why the kids of the greatest

professional athletes and businessmen in the world never amounted to anything near as great as their parents? It's because they didn't have what it took. They didn't have the 'it' factor that their father had. They didn't understand that being born with a high profile name doesn't mean shit. What does mean shit is you getting down and grinding your way to whatever the hell it is you want to do.

Want to go vacation on Cabo every month for the rest of your life? Want to date beautiful women for the rest of your life? Want to build a business that succeeds at a high level? Well make it fucking happen. Aww, your mom and dad told you that that lifestyle would never be possible. That's a bunch of bullshit. Anything's possible if you put your head down and plug forward. The major corporations and entities that exist in the world today were once nothing more than ideas. They were a means to solve a problem that people in the world had.

Impossible? That doesn't mean a damn thing. Impossible is the dumbest word I've ever heard. You want impossible? Look at the moon around 10PM tonight. You know what's impossible? Someone ever building something that would allow humans to get there. There's no way that anyone could ever build something that would take a human being all the way up to that moon right? Wrong, it happened.

Ooo but you aren't *smart* enough? You weren't born with the intelligence or IQ that these other guys possess? Guess what, Les Brown was labeled educable mentally retarded when he was in grade school. He now has a net worth in the tens of millions. Les Brown took control of his life and became an alpha male.

Chris Wallace - the man whose life was played out in *The Pursuit of Happiness* - was homeless with a young child to take care of. He could've given up. He could've given in to the struggles of his life and become content with moving from homeless shelter to homeless shelter. But he didn't. He made a decision that his life wasn't going to turn out that way. He made a decision that his life wasn't going to be controlled by anybody but himself. Chris Wallace took control of his life and became an alpha male.

This isn't a book to tell you about how to build a business or this and that about what you need to do to improve your life. I mention those men only because they became alpha males and reaped the rewards of it. I mention those men because they didn't care where they were, they just found out where they wanted to go and got there. I also mention those men so you can realize what becoming an alpha male can do for you and your life. These men realized that they had the ability to take control of their lives and did it to their full ability. You have that same ability to take control of your own life.

If you're weak, if you can't handle the truth, then go away. If you don't have the desire to become an alpha male and do what you need to do then there's no reason for you to begin reading this book in the first place. If, however, you're ready to take control of your life and become the alpha male you desire to be then you're in for a treat.

Some of you keep crying about your job, your finances, your relationships. SHUT UP! Stop fucking complaining. Alpha males don't complain. When something needs fixed they don't spend their time complaining about the fact that it needs fixed. They don't seek out the condolences of other people.

Alpha males don't act like victims. If something was done wrongly to them or if someone backstabs them, they move on. They don't downgrade the person or waste their time complaining about what they did to them. They move on and learn from it. They understand that times are going to come where things like this happen and there is nothing you can do about it but learn from it and move on.

We've defined within this chapter the type of person that an alpha male is, now it's time to become one. It's time to get your shit together and start making the moves necessary to become an alpha male.

To check out the rest of *"Alpha Male: Stop Being a P#ssy, Become an Alpha Male - The Ultimate Guide to Attract Women & Achieve Massive Success In Life "*, **go to Amazon and look for it right now!**

Ps: You'll find many more books like these under my name, William Wyatt.
Don't miss them! Here's a short list:

- Emotional Intelligence
- Communication Skills
- Persuasion Power
- 7 Reason Why You SUCK at Sales (And What to do About It)

- Introverts Will Rule the World
- Self Discipline NOW

- Charisma NOW
- Much, much more!

About the Author

William Wyatt is a serial entrepreneur, having founded several companies throughout his life. He focuses his energies on the achievement of individual success, as he believes every man and women on earth were born to be successful.

He has lead numerous teams within his business career, maximizing each and every time the effects of proper management. During the past two decades he has acquired a powerful set of leadership tools, which in turn allowed him to take his communication & social skills to the next level.

Being a big believer of the importance of self development in every area of life, he's constantly expanding his knowledge and testing out new things. He enjoys sharing experiences with other business leaders as well, as he's certain that surrounding yourself with the right people can indeed skyrocket your life.

Born in 1964, William has a curious mind. He is student of history, always willing to research the lives of great individuals. He defines himself as a "student of infinite mentors", finding in all of them valuable knowledge to be incorporated.

William enjoys publishing books that can make a real impact in people's lives. If you have any suggestions or would like to have a certain subject covered in a future book, please send an email to williamwyattbooks@gmail.com and we will get back to you.

Thanks for reading!